A HOW-TO BOOK FOR BAND AND CHORAL DIRECTORS

The Music Director's

GUIDE TO THE DRUMSET

BY FRANK MAY

CONTENTS

0-7935-1791-5

Hal Leonard Publishing Corporation

7777 West Bluemound Road P.O. Box 13819 Milwaukee, WI 53213

Copyright © 1992 by HAL LEONARD PUBLISHING CORPORATION
International Copyright Secured   All Rights Reserved

For all works contained herein:
Unauthorized copying, arranging, adapting, recording or public performance is an infringement of copyright.
Infringers are liable under the law.

ABOUT THE AUTHOR

Frank May began playing the drums when he was a very young child. That early start has enabled him to gain experience in virtually every field of drumming. At school he was in the Drum Corps and a jazz band; later, during military service, he played in various army bands.

He studied with prominent percussionists around the world and graduated from the Advanced School of Contemporary Music, in Toronto.

For more than thirty years he has played with internationally known jazz musicians, singers, pop stars, and dancers; with all kinds of acts in night clubs, theaters, television and recording studios; and in opera and symphony orchestras.

He enjoys teaching and he is constantly searching for better and quicker ways to enlighten his students; either in private lessons or by giving drum clinics.

He has written two other drum books: *The QUINTESSENCE OF DRUMMING* and *The 8 WEEK DRUM COURSE.*

A NOTE TO TEACHERS

Are the following problems familiar to you?

- The drummer plays the written notes, but it doesn't sound right.

- The drummer reads a little, but can't read a drum chart.

- The drummer never varies the beat.

- The drummer can't play a drum fill.

- The drummer loses his or her place in the music.

- The drummer has trouble concentrating.

Over the years many music teachers have come to me for help with these and other problems. I begin by pointing out that the ability to play in a big band has always been a problem for most drummers. Rarely do drum students learn how to read charts during private lessons. Often, when a young person starts taking drum lessons, he or she only wants to learn how to play rock - in a hurry. So, the student is given exercises to develop the hands (rudiments), shown how to read snare drum and bass drum notes, then taught some rock beats. Many drum teachers themselves were never taught chart reading, or have big band experience - so *they* don't teach it. The result is that inadequately instructed drum students become problems for the schools to deal with, and the music teachers have to cope with drummers who are not sufficiently prepared to play in stage bands.

The music teachers that have come to me for advice, are always surprised to find how, with a minimum of instruction, they quickly achieve better results from their drummers. And it was these 'satisfied customers' who suggested I should write a book, specifically for music teachers, and include all the material that has helped them.

Music teachers don't, usually, have enough free time to take drum lessons, so there is a need for a book to help them solve these unique problems. This book is my attempt to fulfill that need, and based on past results, I feel confident that it will prove to be a godsend to music teachers.

HOW TO USE THIS BOOK

During band rehearsals, teachers are usually too busy to spend much time with individual players. Consequently, the drummer is often left with nothing to do while the teacher takes care of the section problems. Therefore, teachers need material that is simple to play and easy to understand, so that the drummer's time is put to good use. Then, when the drummer is given a simple, yet adequate, rhythm, he or she can play along with the band. By gradually building on a simple beat, the drummer will soon be playing the rhythm you want.

Problem:

Your drummer can't play the written rhythm:

Solution:

1. Turn to the page that has that basic rhythm and you will find simplified beats that any young drummer could play.

2. Start at the top with the easiest substitute rhythm and let the drummer work down the page to the most suitable beat.

Problem:

The drum part is unclear as to which rhythm should be played.

Solution:

1.   Decide which rhythm you think would sound and 'feel' better for that tune - rock, jazz, or shuffle, etc.

2.   Turn to the page that shows the rhythm you want, then let the drummer start at the top with the easiest substitute and work down the page to the most suitable beat.

Problem:

The drummer can't play a drum 'fill'.

Solution:

1.   Turn to the page that shows drum 'fills'.

2.   Choose a triplet 'fill' for a jazz or swing tune, or a sixteenth note 'fill' for a rock or Latin tune.

HOW TO TUNE THE DRUMS

To produce beautiful music *all* the instruments must be in tune. This would seem to be obvious, but apparently it is not obvious to some drummers and music teachers, who either don't think to tune their drums, or don't know how to tune them.

You should decide the type of sound you would like <u>before</u> you start tuning the drums. Usually drummers prefer a tight, crisp-sounding snare drum and a fairly tight bass drum; this applies to most kinds of music. The tom-toms are usually tuned to a high pitch for jazz and a lower pitch for rock. Once you know the sound you want the next step is to buy the right drum heads (skins) to produce that sound. There are many different kinds of heads but all you need to know are the three basic types:

- **White coated** - Essential for playing brushes; medium to high pitch sound.

- **Clear** - Medium to high pitch sound. <u>Always</u> use a clear <u>bottom head</u> on the snare drum.

- **Hydraulic** (Two-ply, oil-filled) - Low pitch, dark sound.

The top head controls the pitch, bounce, and clarity. The bottom head controls the volume and tone. Heads should be replaced if they become dented, pin-holed or split.

To obtain the best sound, the drums should be played one or two inches off-center - this includes the bass drum beater.

- <u>The drums should be tuned to **INDEFINITE** pitches</u>.

Only on rare occasions would you want a definite pitch like 'D' or 'G'. However, the pitches should be of equal distance (steps) apart. A good way to do this is: starting with the small tom-tom and decending to the floor tom-tom, try to *approximate* the first three notes of 'Three blind mice.'

Tuning the batter head (playing surface) - Start by tuning the snare drum, then the small tom, medium tom, floor tom and lastly the bass drum. Place the drum on a flat surface. Take both heads off the drum. Clean away any dust and, if necessary, smooth the edge of the shell where the head will touch. Dip the end of each tension rod (1/4") in petroleum jelly. Then replace the head and *hand tighten* each tension rod. Using the drum key, and working in a clockwise direction, give each tension rod <u>three turns.</u> Some drummers work from one rod to its opposite, then to the one next to it, then opposite again etc., either way is acceptable. Press down in the center of the head with both hands, then give each rod <u>one more turn.</u> Push down in the center of the head again, and keep repeating <u>one turn at a time</u> until the desired playing tension is reached.

Using a stick, tap the head one inch in from each lug to make sure the pitch is the same at all of them. Adjust, if necessary, by tightening the tension rod with the lowest pitch a <u>half turn</u> at a time.

Tuning the bottom head - This is done in the same manner as the batter head. Turn the drum over and place it on the drum stool, or a folded towel, so that you hear only the head you are tuning.

Repeat the procedure for each drum.

Selecting the relative tensions - To obtain the desired sound and bounce.

- **Both heads tight** - crisp, clear, high pitch, lots of bounce.
- **Top tight, bottom looser** - lower pitch, lots of bounce.
- **Top looser, bottom tighter** - fatter sound, less bounce.
- **Both heads loose** - flat, dead sound, bad projection and poor bounce.

Snares - The snares should be tight but not choked and all the strands must lay flat on the head or they will buzz.

Muffling - **Don't** stuff the bass drum with blankets or pillows!
　　　　　　　Don't put tape on the heads!

Control the overtones - don't eliminate them entirely. Pre-cut 'O' rings - made of clear mylar (plastic) which is about one and a half inches wide - can be purchased and laid on the top head of each drum next to the rim (they can be removed when not needed). For the bass drum use thin strips of felt, about three inches wide, place them against the <u>inside</u> of each head, half way between the center and the rim and stretching from top to bottom. They are held in place by the head and the rim. An even better sound can be obtained if you tape a two inch wide, by a half to one inch thick, circle of foam around the <u>inside</u> circumference of the batter head. The commercial version of this - Remo Muff'ls - is better because it is held in place by a plastic tray.

HOW TO SET-UP THE DRUMS

Stool - The first thing to find is the most comfortable height at which to sit. Whether you sit high or low is of little importance, but it will be less tiring if you can avoid holding your arms out, or up, to play on the drums and cymbals. Also, it is possible to avoid reaching and stretching, (except for the crash cymbal) by having the drums close together, and not too high.

Hi-hat - The hi-hat is played with the left foot. The hi-hat cymbals should be four to six inches above the snare drum; this is to prevent the sticks hitting each other when playing on the hi-hat with crossed hands.

Floor tom-tom - The floor tom-tom should be close to the leg you use to play the bass drum. The floor tom should be at the same level as the snare drum or slightly lower; so that you don't hit the rim.

Snare drum and **Small tom-tom** - These drums should be directly in front of the drummer and close to each other with the **Medium tom-tom** an inch or two to the right of the small tom-tom. Both the tom-toms are two or three inches higher than the snare drum and angled towards the drummer.

Ride cymbal - This is on the right side of the **Bass drum** (to the right of the medium tom-tom) and close enough to play without stretching, and angled for ease of playing.

Crash cymbal - This is to the left and forward of the small tom-tom and high enough to prevent it hitting the tom-tom when struck hard. It is angled only slightly to leave the edge in a position to be 'crashed.' The crash cymbal should be the only part of the drum set that the drummer must reach out to play.

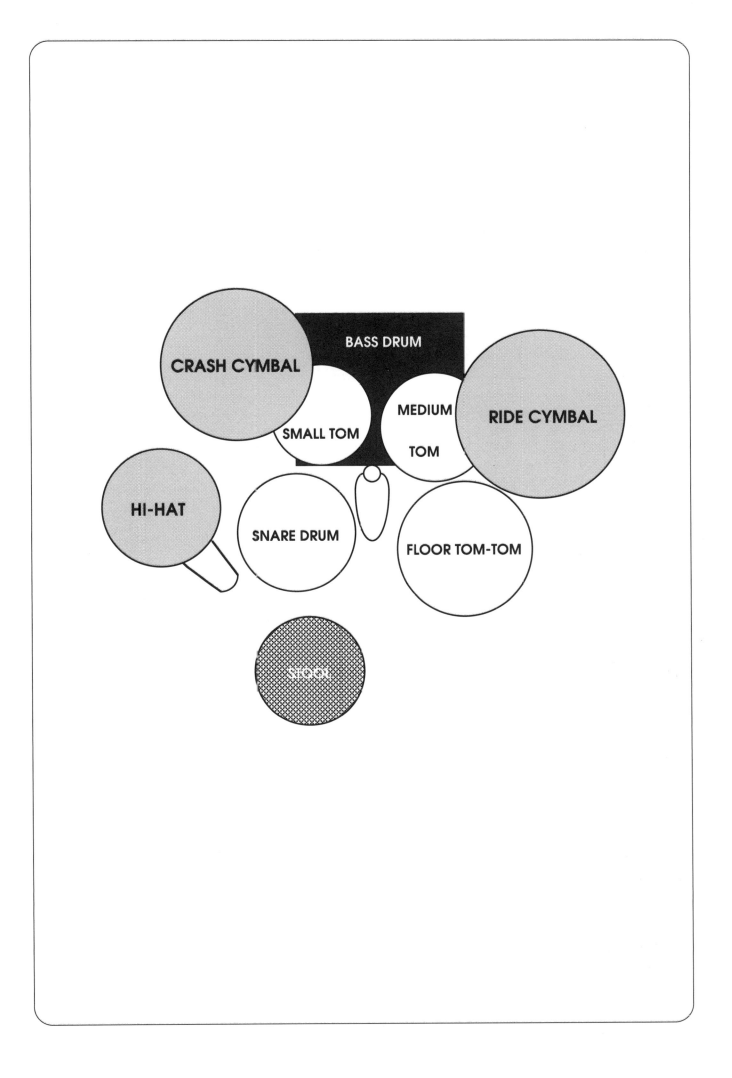

HOW TO READ DRUM NOTATION

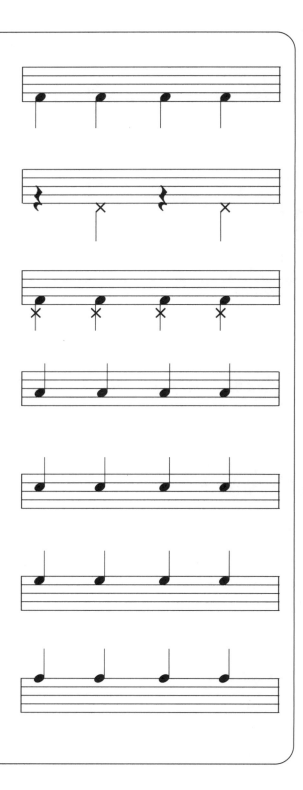

Bass drum - Written in the bottom space. Always played softly, except for rock, disco and marches.

Hi-hat - Written below the staff. Played with the foot. Try to get a strong, but short 'chick' sound.

Bass drum and hi-hat - Played together.

Floor tom-tom - Written in the space second from the bottom.

Snare drum - Written in the space third from the bottom.

Medium tom-tom - Written in the top space.

Small tom-tom - Written on the top line. Additional tom-toms can be written on any unused line or space. Higher pitches on ledger lines and lower pitches on the staff.

Cymbals - Can be written above the staff, on the top line or in the top space. Cymbals are indicated by a cross for all notes except whole and half notes, which are written as diamonds.

Closed (buzz) rolls - Written as abbreviated thirty-second notes.

Cymbal rolls

Open hi-hat - Indicated by H.H. or HI-HAT and a circle over each note. Played partially open to produce a long sound when the cymbals rattle together.

Closed hi-hat - Indicated by H.H. or HI-HAT and a plus sign over each note. A short 'chick' sound.

Hi-hat played with sticks

Sounds like:

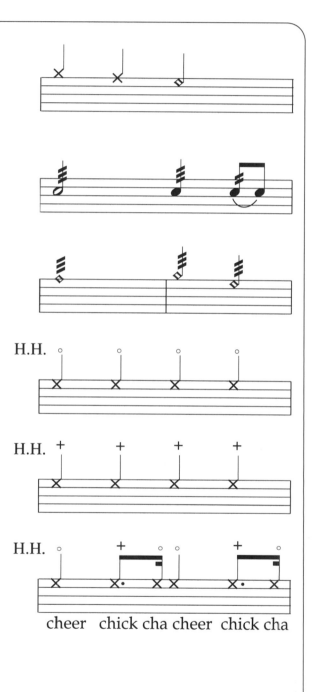

cheer chick cha cheer chick cha

HOW DRUMMERS COUNT

The counts that are in brackets are not played, but they should be said out loud when the drummer is practicing, and silently counted during performance.

The closed (BUZZ) roll is executed in the following manner:

1. Hold the sticks firmly but not *too* tight; they must be able to bounce freely.

2. As the stick strikes the drum a slight downward pressure is applied to produce several fast rebounds - the BUZZ.

3. Play sixteenth notes with the wrists and alternate R L R L.

4. Play evenly - both hands must sound the same.

5. At very slow tempos it will sound like: BUZZ BUZZ BUZZ etc., but at faster tempos it should sound like: BUZZZZZZZZZZZ.

6. All rolls finish with a single tap.

Interpretation

Often, individual rolls are written when the composer really intended a long roll to be played. If whole note rolls appear in each measure, but they are not joined by ties, it is usually a mistake and they should be played as one continuous roll. It most often happens when a series of whole, half or quarter note rolls appear together.

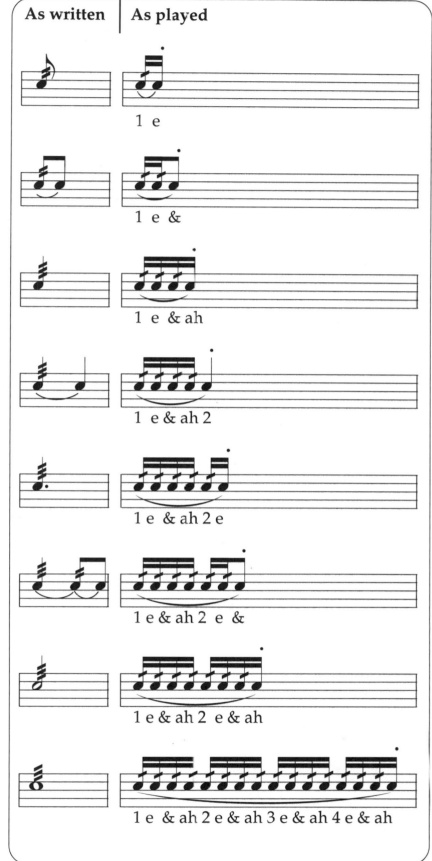

As written	As played
	1 e
	1 e &
	1 e & ah
	1 e & ah 2
	1 e & ah 2 e
	1 e & ah 2 e &
	1 e & ah 2 e & ah
	1 e & ah 2 e & ah 3 e & ah 4 e & ah

HOW TO PLAY DRUM FIGURES

Figures are groups of two or more notes, usually accented, that add rhythmic emphasis to the music.

There are two types of figures:

1. **Ensemble figures:**
   Written on the staff and are played by the whole band including the drummer.

   As played at first (while learning the part): Both hands together, right hand on the ride cymbal and left hand on the snare drum, while the bass drum and hi-hat continue unchanged:

   As played correctly: Once the drummer is aware of how the figure is supposed to sound, he or she can play the figure, as shown, with an added 'fill' and the bass drum and crash cymbal (14" to 18") played together:

   R = Right hand.   L = Left hand.

2. **Section figures:**
   Written above the staff as a 'cue' line. They are the notes played by some of the band, such as the brass or reed sections, and can usually be omitted by the drummer.

Remember:

> *Section figures must only be played if the flow of the rhythm is not interrupted.*

As played: The section figure should be played independently with the left hand while the right hand maintains the cymbal pattern (rhythm).

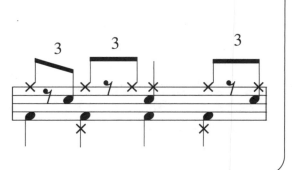

HOW TO PLAY DRUM 'FILLS'
(for any rhythm)

In many stage band arrangements there are places that are left open for the drummer to play ad-lib 'fills'. These openings can vary from a single beat to a measure or more, but usually they are less than one measure.

A 'fill' is most often used to set up a figure or to fill any holes during a figure.

The 'fills' shown on this page are those used most often by professional drummers. They are effective, yet easy to play.

The <u>one beat</u> 'fill' and the <u>two note</u> 'fills' (lines one and two) can be used in any type of music.

The sixteenth note 'fills' are suitable for rock or Latin music.

The triplet 'fills' are suitable for jazz, swing, or with the shuffle rhythm.

Remember:

Jazz is played with a triplet feel and eighth notes are played like triplets without the middle note.

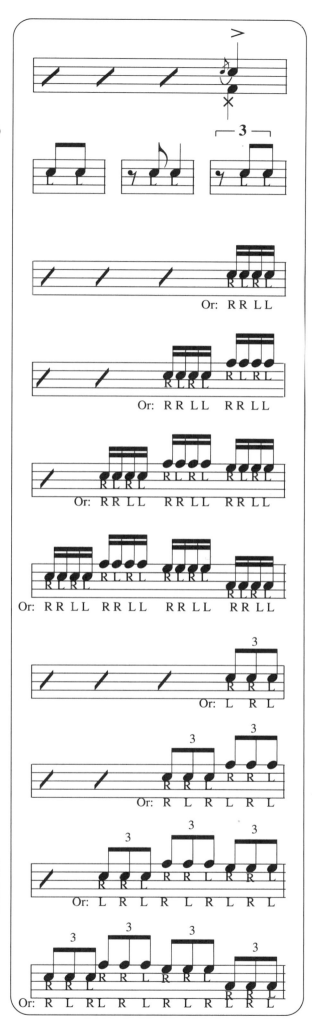

HOW TO APPROACH A DRUM PART

Drum music is very different from music for melodic instruments. The drum part is designed to give the drummer freedom, so that he or she can concentrate on keeping the time steady; playing with 'feeling'; and making the music 'swing'. However, it requires the drummer to listen to all the other instruments and to be creative. The drummer is, therefore, permitted to contribute his or her personal interpretation of the music. This is done through the use of 'fills', accents and the choice of which cymbal or drum to play.

Many drummers and music teachers are unaware that the drum part in a stage band (big band) is only a guide, and is not meant to be played 'as written.' Of course, there are places in most stage band drum parts when a 'figure' must match, exactly, what the other instruments are playing. (Note: The percussion part in a *concert band*, is usually more specific and should, normally, be played 'as written').

The big band arranger is really saying to the drummer:

- I want you to play a jazz rhythm (or rock, or Latin, etc.,) so, play something appropriate throughout.

- Here . . . is where I want you to play the rhythm.

- Here . . . is where you don't play.

- Here . . . are the accents I want you to play.

- Here . . . are the dynamics I want you to play.

- And here . . . is where I want you to play a 'figure', and perhaps a 'fill' that suits the music.

- Play musically, have fun, and the most important thing of all - keep steady time.

HOW TO GET RESULTS

Most rhythms, except for some Latin and jazz rhythms, are usually played on the hi-hat for the first chorus, and then moved to the ride cymbal (biggest cymbal) for the solos and ensemble choruses.

In 4/4 swing or jazz, the bass drum is usually played 'two-in-the-bar' (1st and 3rd beats) for the first chorus, then 'four-in-the-bar' (1st, 2nd, 3rd, and 4th beats) for the rest of the tune, and sometimes - but not often - coming back to 'two-in-the-bar' for the last chorus.

Where there is an accent to be played on a cymbal, it should be played on a crash cymbal (14 to 18 inches in diameter) and the bass drum should be played simultaneously.

In jazz or swing, the snare drum is rarely played on the second and fourth beats. Instead, the left hand is used to play ad-lib accents and 'fills'. The exception is Dixieland jazz, where '2' and '4' are often played lightly on the snare drum.

Encourage the drummer to listen to the bass player. When the bassist plays 2 or 4 beats-in-the-bar the drummer should play the same beats on the bass drum; during rock tunes play, on the bass drum, a rhythm similar to what the bassist is playing.

For jazz, ask the drummer to play the bass drum softly, or not to play it at all.

For rock, disco and marches the bass drum should be loud, but for all other kinds of music the bass drum should be 'felt' rather than heard.

For soft rock, ballads, and some jazz, the left stick can be laid flat on the snare drum, with the butt end across the rim, and played as a 'rim click' on the 2nd and 4th beats.

Teach your drummer how to count measures. By counting two measures, then four, eight, twelve and sixteen; as follows:

<u>1</u>2 3 4 <u>2</u>2 3 4 <u>3</u>2 3 4 <u>4</u>2 3 4

This will help - even if the drummer can't read the part - to at least know where you are in the music. Then you can give directions, such as: play until the 16th measure then don't play for the next four measures, or, when we get to bar twelve, hit the cymbal on the first beat, etc.

HOW TO BACK-UP VOCALS AND SOLOS

Every musician in the band plays an important role when working with a soloist, whether they are playing harmony or background figures. One of the most important musicians is the piano player, who is essentially the accompanist for the soloist. It is the pianist or keyboard player who supplies the chords and notes that are necessary for the soloist to sing or play in tune. However, when the singer or instrumentalist steps forward to perform, it is the drummer that the soloist depends upon - more than any other musician in the band.

• Drums can be very offensive instruments if played without taste; therefore, the ability to play musically is a major quality for the drummer to strive for.

• The drummer should never be obtrusive or overplay. The vocalist, soloist, or even the quietest instrument in the band, should not be drowned out.

• Make the drummer aware of the dynamics and have him or her use sticks, brushes or mallets in their correct place.

• Encourage the drummer to listen to various kinds of music such as country, Latin, jazz, and funk, etc., and to take note of how the drummer plays in each situation. Listening is the best way for a drummer to learn how to play any style of music.

• Tell the drummer to listen to the singer or soloist and to play appropriate 'fills' and accents, when needed, to motivate, drive, or excite the soloist.

• Tonal colors are important. The drummer can play many simple things that are effective:

- Use a cymbal that best suits the situation: low pitched (big) cymbals when backing high pitched instruments; high pitched (smaller) cymbals when backing low pitched instruments. Contrast is usually better than a blend of sounds.

- Use brushes for ballads or play lightly with sticks.

- Change from brushes to sticks as a song builds to a climax.

- Try to use sticking to suit the phrase. Example: RLRL sounds different to RRLL and RLRR sounds different to both of them.

• Vocalists, choral groups, and instrumental soloists need to feel confident that the drummer will provide them with the security of a steady tempo. If the time is steady the soloist will feel relaxed, comfortable, and will perform better.

• When you are busy working with a section of the band and the drummer is not doing anything, have him or her practice troublesome parts of the music on a practice pad, in tempo with a metronome.

HOW TO PLAY BRUSHES

Wire brushes are used in dance music, jazz, and Latin music; their main purpose is to play the rhythm quietly. Brushes are ideal for producing tonal colors and delicate sounds in any style of music. There are many ways to play brushes but it's the end result that counts. Shown below are two of the easiest brush patterns. The grip for brushes is the same as for sticks.

• Use telescopic brushes and retract the right brush a little to produce a clear beat. The left brush can be opened wide to produce the 'steam' sound.

• Leave the snares on the drum when playing in large groups, but for trios - or when backing singers or piano solos - release the snares. This is to prevent the snares buzzing when set-off by low pitched notes - especially from the bass player.

• Use only the top half-inch of the wire strands for light and clean sounds. For 'fat' accents use two or three inches of the strands.

• The right hand plays the jazz rhythm:

• The left hand slides the brush from side to side making a continuous 'steam' sound.

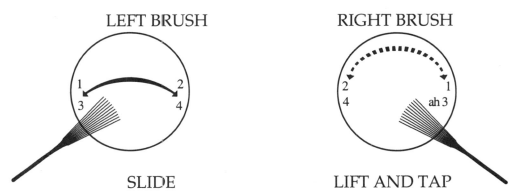

LEFT BRUSH. Start with the hands apart. The left brush is <u>on</u> the left side of the drum head at the count of '1' and slides to the right side of the drum reaching it on the count of '2'. It continues sliding and returns to the left side of the drum by the count of '3', and continues back again to the right side of the drum reaching it on the count of '4'. There is no break in the motion and the brush remains on the drum at all times.

RIGHT BRUSH. The right brush taps '1' on the right side of the drum head and is lifted and carried to the left side of the drum to tap '2'. It is lifted and carried to the right side of the drum to tap 'ah 3', lifted again and carried to the left side to tap '4'. Then it is carried back to the right side again to tap 'ah 1' and continues in this fashion.

3/4 TIME. A simple brush pattern for waltzes is to start with the hands crossed and both brushes on the drum head. On the count of '1' slide both hands across the drum, in opposite directions, and when the right brush reaches the right side of the drum it taps '2', '3'. Lift and cross both hands again and continue in this manner.

Beguine

The beguine is played on the snare drum with the snares off. It is often played with the left stick laid flat on the drum - the butt end of the stick plays on the rim and the right stick plays on the drum.

It can also be played with both sticks on the drum.

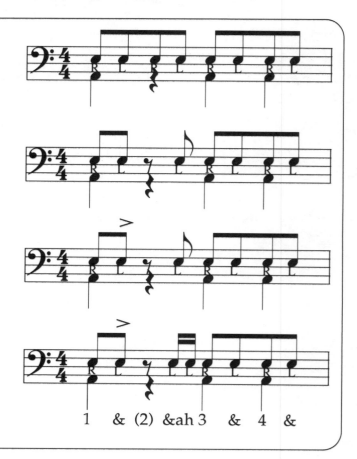

Rhumba

The rhumba is similar to the beguine but is a little faster. It is played with the snares off. The left stick is laid flat on the drum - the butt end of the stick plays on the rim and the right stick plays on the drum.

It can also be played, as shown in this third example, by playing the right stick on the shell (side) of the floor tom-tom or on the cow bell.

Bossa Nova

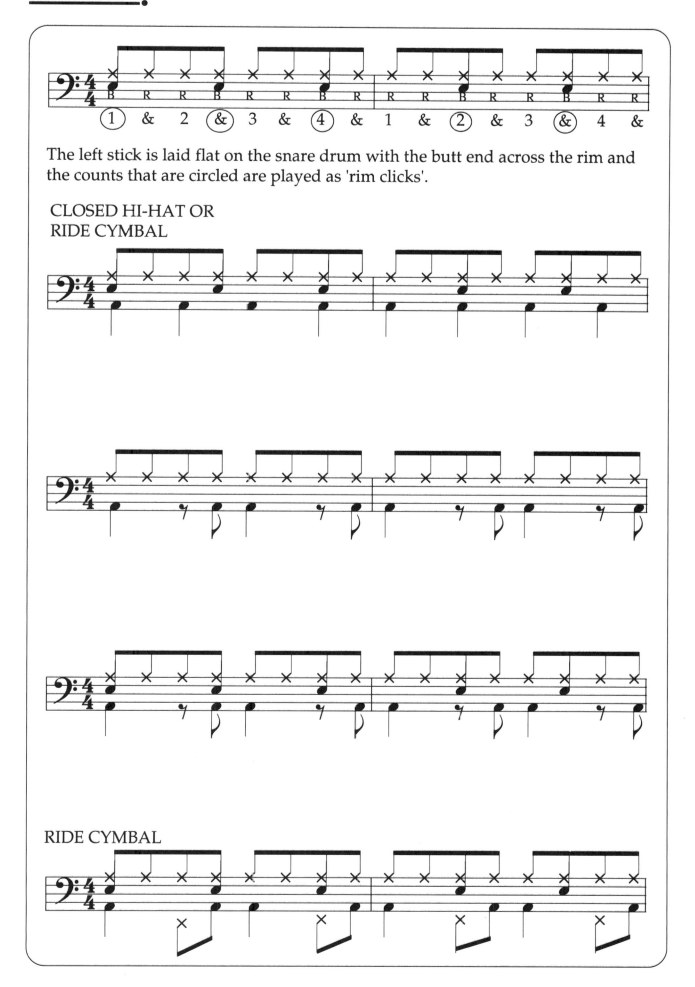

The left stick is laid flat on the snare drum with the butt end across the rim and the counts that are circled are played as 'rim clicks'.

CLOSED HI-HAT OR
RIDE CYMBAL

RIDE CYMBAL

Disco.

Remember:

> *The bass drum should be played louder for disco.*

Played on closed hi-hat. Come back to the snare drum with the right stick for '2' and '4'.

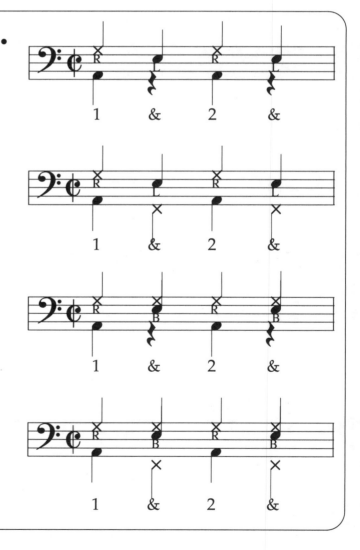

1 e & ah etc.................................

Fast 2
(polka, can-can, charleston etc.)

Played on closed hi-hat or ride cymbal.

Jazz, swing or Dixieland

Play on hi-hat as you open and close it.

o = open - just enough so that the cymbals produce a 'steam' sound.
+ = closed.

For slow tempos.

For medium to fast tempos.

Lay the left stick flat on the snare drum with the butt end across the rim and play a 'click' on '2' and '4'.

Latin
(montuno, mambo, son, guaracha etc.)

Use the shoulder (thick part) of the sticks and play on the edge of the hi-hat cymbals.

Play on the cow bell or the bell of the ride cymbal.

Cow bell or bell of ride cymbal.

Afro-Cuban

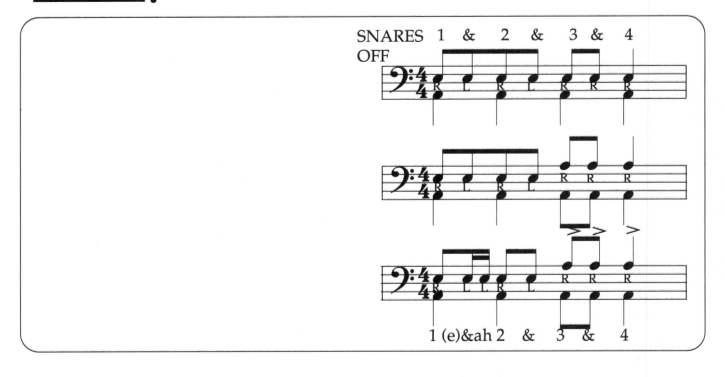

Cha-Cha

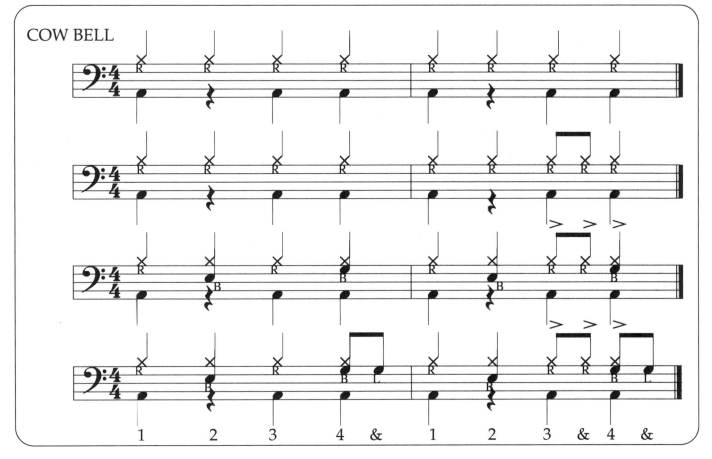

Merengue

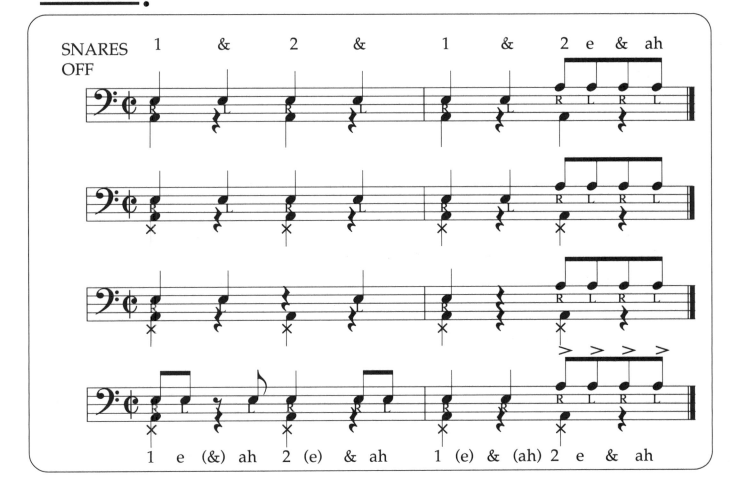

Calypso

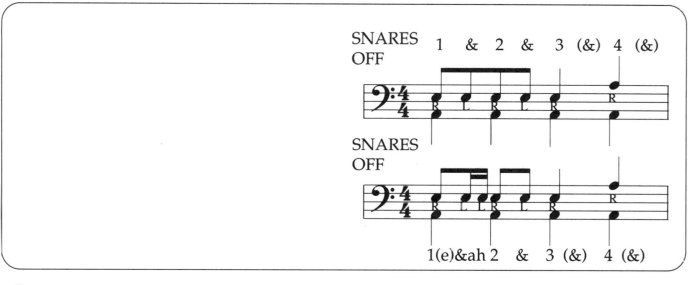

Reggae

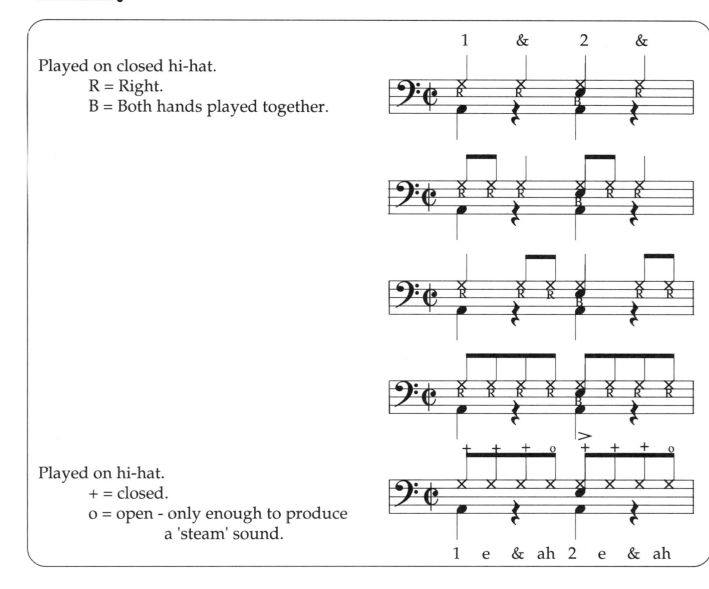

Played on closed hi-hat.
    R = Right.
    B = Both hands played together.

Played on hi-hat.
    + = closed.
    o = open - only enough to produce
              a 'steam' sound.

Rock.

R = right.
B = both hands played together.

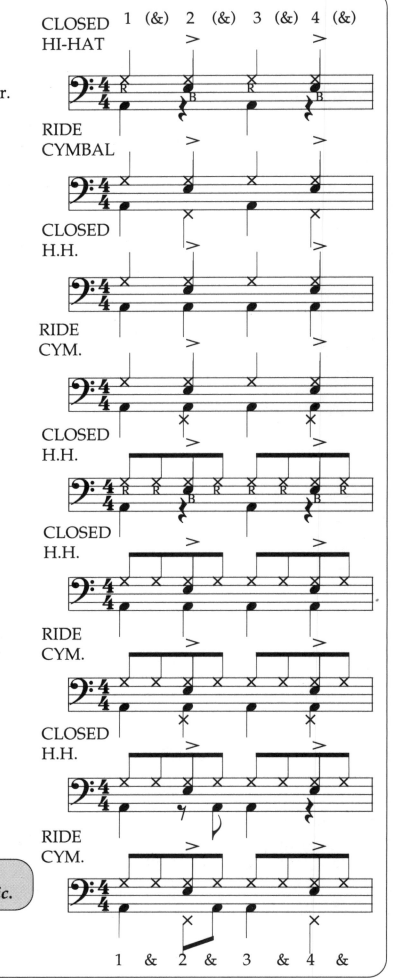

Remember:

The bass drum should be played louder for rock music.

Samba.

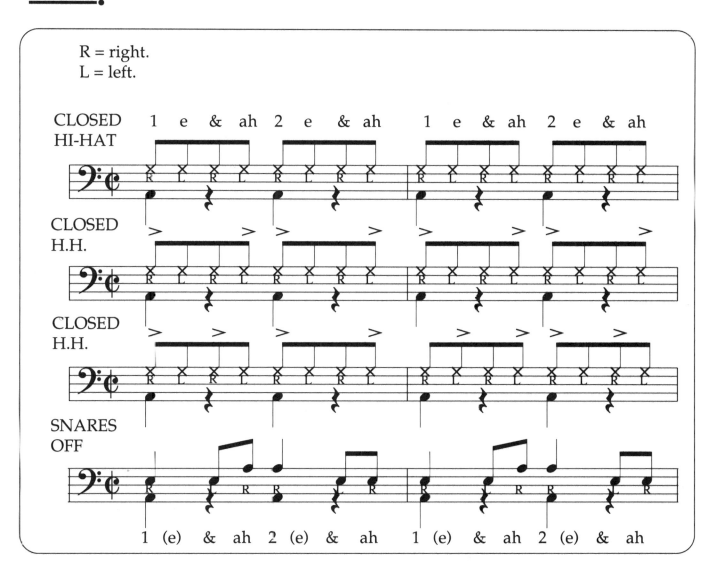

Shuffle.

R = right.
B = both hands played together.

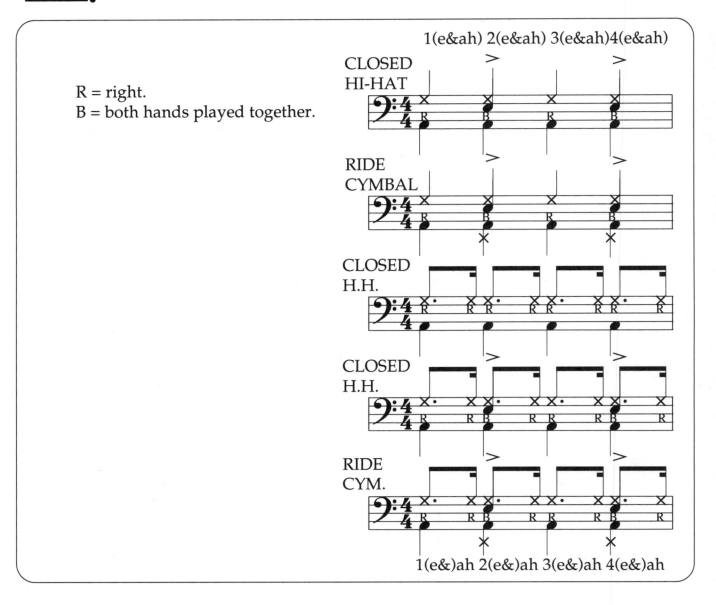

Triplet rock .

R = right.
B = both hands played together.

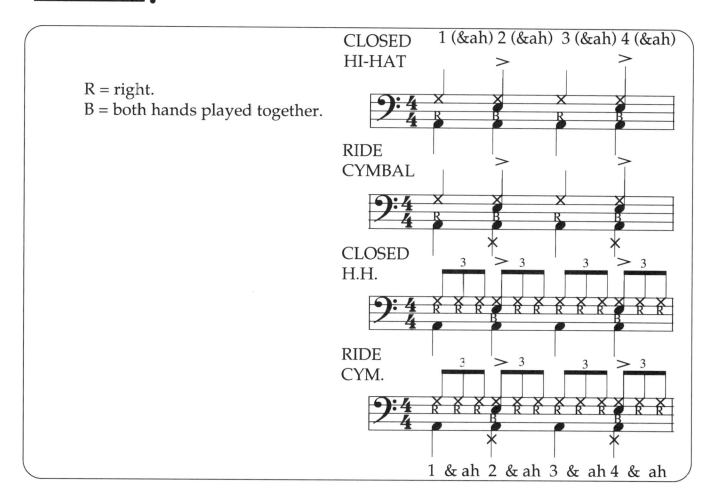

12/8 (very slow rock) .

R = right.
B = both hands played together.

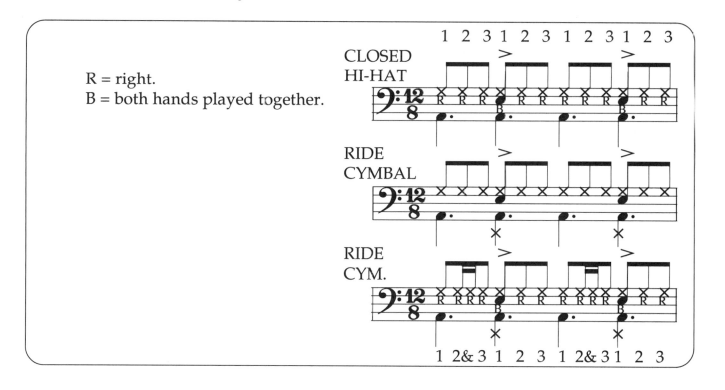

Waltz

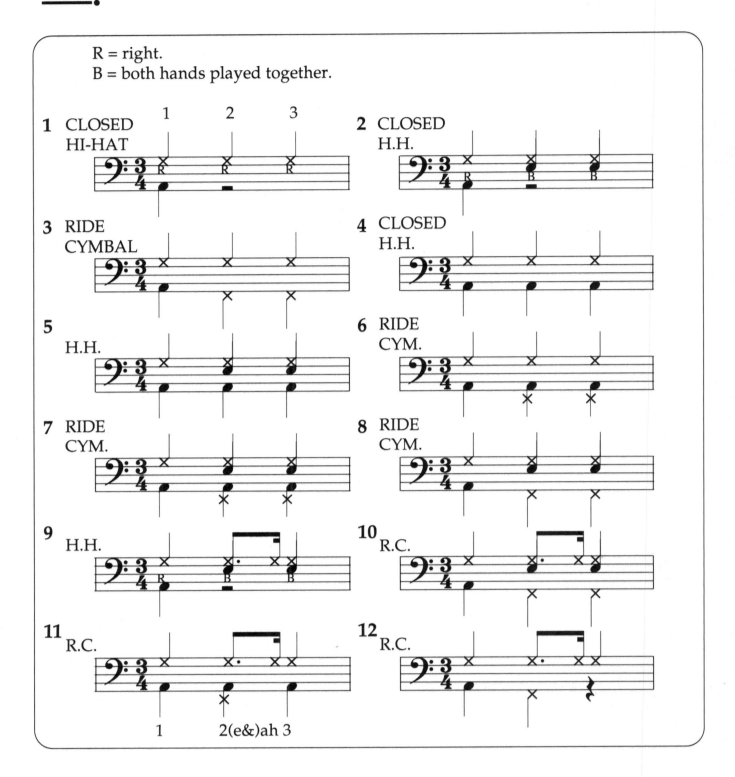